THE CELTIC WAY OF LIFE

'excellent for Irish American students and for the general reader as well'
Irish Echo

'a collection of historical facts, traditional legends and myths, illustrated with drawings and with photographs of archaeological findings of ornaments, weapons, statues and pottery . . . a remarkable book'
Sunday Independent

THE O'BRIEN PRESS
EXPLORING SERIES

OTHER BOOKS IN THE SERIES

Exploring the Book of Kells
George Otto Simms

Brendan the Navigator
George Otto Simms

St Patrick
George Otto Simms

The World of Colmcille
Mairé ad Ashe FitzGerald

The Vikings in Ireland
Morgan Llywelyn

THE CELTIC WAY OF LIFE

Curriculum Development Unit

Reconstruction drawings: Josip Lizatovic

THE O'BRIEN PRESS
DUBLIN

This revised edition first published 1998 by The O'Brien Press Ltd.
20 Victoria Road, Dublin 6, Ireland.
Tel +353-1-4923333 Fax +353-1-4922777
e-mail books@obrien.ie Internet www.obrien.ie
Reprinted 2000.
Original edition published 1976 by The O'Brien Press Ltd. Reprinted 1977,
1978, 1980, 1982, 1984, 1986, 1987, 1988, 1990, 1992, 1994, 1997.

ISBN 0-86278-563-4

British Library Cataloguing-in-publication Data
A catalogue reference for this book is available from the British Library.

16 17 18 19 20
00 01 02 03 04 05

The Curriculum Development Unit was established in 1972. It was funded by
the City of Dublin Vocational Education Committee and managed jointly by
the City of Dublin Vocational Education Committee at Trinity College,
Dublin, and the Department of Education, with Anton Trant as Unit
Director. This book formed part of the humanities curriculum.

The humanities team:
Tony Crooks, co-ordinator; Nora Godwin, Agnes McMahon.
The original edition of this book was prepared by Agnes McMahon.

Typesetting: The O'Brien Press Ltd.
Revisions: Mairéad Ashe FitzGerald
Layout: William Healy
Printing: Biddles Ltd.

C O N T E N T S

CONTENTS

CHAPTER 1

WHO WERE THE CELTS?

INTRODUCTION

The Celts came from Central Europe, an area east of the river Rhine and north of the Alps – the lands now called Bavaria and Bohemia. They were a farming people, brave and warlike, and from time to time groups of them would set out to find new lands to settle. They spread out in all directions, into France and Spain in the west, into Ireland and Britain in the north, into Italy in the south, into Greece and Turkey in the east. From about 450 BC to 250 BC they were the most powerful people in Europe.

Historians are not certain when the Celts first came to Ireland, but it was probably about 300 BC. They were not the first settlers, in fact Ireland had been inhabited since about 6000 BC, but they did change the pattern of life throughout the country. They brought in new customs and skills, especially the ability to make tools and weapons from iron, and they may have introduced the distinctive Celtic language.

Because the Celts developed a knowledge of iron-working,

Map-making began in the Middle East, first with the Egyptians and then the Greeks. Ireland was not on the main trading routes, but would still have had contact with European countries. In the second century AD, a Greek map-maker called Claudius Ptolemy plotted the position of Ireland and collected information about the country. This map has been drawn from the information that Ptolemy gave in his writings. Reproduced from a woodcut made in Strasbourg, Austria, in 1513 (from a manuscript in the National Library of Ireland).

we call the period from about 450 BC onwards the Celtic Iron Age. Their material culture is known as La Tène after a great site of that name in Switzerland where thousands of Celtic weapons and other objects were found in the last century. These objects were decorated in a distinctive art-style which we now call La Tène.

Ireland never formed part of the Roman Empire nor did the Vikings start to raid until the eighth century, so the Celtic customs and traditions survived relatively undisturbed until then, even though Christianity was introduced in the fifth century.

Extensive research has been done in Ireland into its Celtic past and there is a lot of detailed knowledge available.

Archaeological remains and excavations tell us a certain amount, and archaeologists can also date timber remains very accurately by the method of tree-ring dating. However, sometimes we need to draw from research into the Continental Celts to fill in gaps – for example, no chariots have been found in Ireland though they have been found on mainland Europe. This may mean that chariots were not used here, even though they are mentioned in the great Irish Celtic epics, or, of course, it may be simply that no remains have yet been found. Also, descriptions of the Celts by Roman writers describe the Continental Celts, but, in the absence of such descriptions of the Irish Celts, we may assume that such habits were also followed by the Celts who came to Ireland.

APPEARANCE

The Celts seem to have been a rather striking people, tall and fair-skinned, with blond or reddish hair. They were very concerned about their appearance and took special care of their hair, which was usually worn fairly long by both men and women. They were fond of jewellery and ornaments and the women probably used cosmetics – berry juice to dye their eyebrows and a herb called *ruaim* to redden their cheeks. Personal hygiene was not neglected; there are references to

Bronze pin, second century BC

people washing and bathing, and using oils and sweet herbs to anoint their bodies after a bath.

It was expected that a host would offer visitors a bath – this was probably necessary as they most likely had walked along muddy roads to reach their destination. Large wooden bath-tubs were used and the water would have been heated by throwing in hot stones. Ash, made by burning bracken and briars, was formed into cakes and used as soap.

There are several descriptions of the Celts by Roman historians, one of whom, Strabo, remarks that the Celts were figure-conscious:

> They try not to become stout and fat-bellied, and any young man who exceeds the standard length of the girdle is fined.

Another Roman commentator, Diodorus Siculus, gives us a more detailed picture. Diodorus was writing about the Celts who lived in the area now known as France, then known as Gaul. Although he refers specifically to the Gauls, his remarks apply to all the Celtic peoples:

> The Gauls are tall in stature and their flesh is very moist and white, while their hair is not only naturally blond, but they also use artificial means to increase this natural quality of colour. For they continually wash their hair with lime-wash and draw it back from their forehead to the crown and to the nape of the neck, with the result that their appearance resembles that of Satyrs or Pans, for the hair is so thickened by this treatment that it differs in no way from a horse's mane. Some shave off the beard, while others cultivate a short beard; the nobles shave the cheeks but let the

9

moustache grow freely so that it covers the mouth. And so when they are eating the moustache becomes entangled in the food, and when they are drinking the drink passes, as it were, through a sort of strainer.

The Celts, unlike the Romans, rarely depicted the human face or body in their art, but in their stories there are many poetic and detailed descriptions of people which show that they loved physical beauty. The colours of hair and eyes are praised, and poets had a tradition of describing the heroes and heroines of their stories in great and poetic detail. In contrast to the rather fearsome picture painted by Diodorus, this is an eighth-century Irish description of a handsome man:

> Froech broke a spray from the tree, and carried it on his back through the water. And this was what Findabhair used to say afterwards of any beautiful thing which she saw, that she thought it more beautiful to see Froech across the dark pool – the body so white and the hair so lovely, the face so shapely, the eye so blue, and he a tender youth without fault or blemish, with face narrow below and above, and he straight and spotless, and the branch with the red berries between the throat and the white face.

A typical safety-pin style brooch, known as a *fibula*, used for fastening garments.

CLOTHING

The Celts wore simple, colourful clothes, using linen and woollen materials which they produced themselves. Men and women both wore tunics. The tunic is a kind of long shirt known in later times as the *léine*. The *brat* was a long cloak worn over the *léine*. Tunics and long cloaks were fastened with pins or brooches. The *brat* worn by nobles was often dyed in beautiful colours, such as crimson, purple or gold. It was often long enough to be wound around the body several times. Sometimes the men wore short, knee-length trousers under their tunics as well; these were referred to as *braccae* by Roman authors. Shoes and sandals were made from leather and tied with thongs.

A simple pin-style brooch.

JEWELLERY

Jewellery was very popular, and rings, bracelets and torcs were worn by both men and women. Brooches too, known as *fibulæ*, were used to fasten cloaks. Most of these ornaments were worked in bronze and show the skill of the bronze-smith in their beautiful designs. They often used red enamel to decorate them. Some bracelets were made of jet or glass. A second-century writer said:

Safety-pin brooch, seen from the back. It is made of cast bronze and was found at Navan Fort, Armagh. It dates to the first century BC.

They wear ornaments of gold, torcs on their necks and bracelets on their arms and wrists, while people of high rank wear dyed garments besprinkled with gold.

Archaeologists have found many of these pins, brooches and torcs, and some of them can be seen in the National Museum in Dublin.

Bronze bracelet, first century AD.

CONVERSATION

The Celts were said to be great talkers and storytellers, although Diodorus Siculus thought that they were boasters as well:

Physically the Gauls are terrifying in appearance, with deep-sounding and very harsh voices. In conversation they use few words and speak in riddles, for the most part hinting at things and leaving a great deal to be understood. They frequently exaggerate with the aim of extolling themselves and diminishing the status of others. They are boasters and threateners and given to bombastic self-dramatisation, and yet they are quick of mind and with good natural ability for learning.

CHAPTER 2

WHERE THEY LIVED

THE COUNTRYSIDE

The Celtic settlers would have been faced with an Irish countryside much wilder and emptier than it is now. Large parts of the country were covered in forests and there were extensive areas of bog and marshland. The oak forests of Ireland were so dense and so highly prized by our ancestors that to this day about 1500 placenames still contain the element *doire* (derry) which means 'oak wood' – for example, Derry, Derryard, Ballinderry. As well as the forest and bogland, there were large open plains where the people grew crops and grazed their animals, and plenty of rivers and lakes to supply fresh water.

From their poetry it is obvious that the Celts loved the countryside. Here is a translation from an Old Irish poem celebrating the arrival of summer:

> Summer has come, healthy and free,
> Whence the brown wood is bent to the ground:
> The slender nimble deer leap,
> And the path of seals is smooth.

A sound of playful breezes in the tops
Of a black oakwood is Drum Daill,
The noble hornless herd runs,
To whom Cuan-wood is a shelter.

The sun smiles over every land -
A parting for me from the brood of cares:
Hounds bark, stags tryst,
Ravens flourish, summer has come!

(Translated by Kuno Meyer)

Wild animals roamed freely through the countryside and there were numerous varieties of bird and fish in the woods. There were also great herds of deer, wild boars with long, dangerous tusks, and even wolves. Flocks of cranes, wild geese and wild swans could be found in the lakes and marsh-lands, and kites (birds of prey of the hawk family), golden eagles and goshawks were much more numerous than they are nowadays.

The Grianán of Aileach, west of Derry, one of the great forts with stone ramparts.

The Celts were a farming people and their homes were isolated rather than being grouped together in towns or villages. There were various types of dwelling places such as hillforts, ringforts and *crannógs,* the remains of which can still be seen in many parts of the country.

HILLFORTS

About fifty or so hilltops in Ireland are encircled by massive ramparts, sometimes up to two or three in a row, with deep ditches all around on the outside. These structures are hillforts and some of them, being enormous, are difficult to see from the ground, but aerial photographs provide a clear view of their features. These great enclosures, we believe, were in use in Celtic times as places of assembly for the tribe, as safe places where people went when the tribe was in danger, or they may have been used as ritual centres on ceremonial occasions. Their origins are lost in the mists of time, but a few have been excavated and we know that they were already being built in the Late Bronze Age (in the last millennium BC). Some of them, like Rathgall in County Wicklow, or Mooghaun in County Clare, would have been old when the Celts first came here but became a central part of the Celtic way of life.

These hillforts are huge structures and they must have required enormous communal effort to build and maintain. The Celts and the people before them must have been very keen on defence. Mooghaun, for example, has three massive ramparts with very deep ditches outside each of them to swallow up any attackers. It encloses an area of nearly twelve hectares and it looks like a powerful tribal centre.

As well as being enormous structures, hillforts are often sited in spectacular settings with commanding views over the countryside. This is the case at the Grianán of Aileach, a great stone fort with four ramparts which encircles a hill in County Donegal. But the fort of Dún Aengus on Inis Mór,

Aran Islands, Dún Aengus, showing the *chevaux-de-frise*.

the largest of the Aran Islands which lie off the Galway coast, is one of the most dramatic of all. It is built at the edge of the steep cliffs on the southern tip of the island. There are three main enclosing walls, the middle wall being surrounded by a *chevaux-de-frise*. This is a broad band of densely-packed limestone pillars, some of them up to a metre in height, wedged into cracks in the limestone; no invaders could have got through it to attack the fort.

The *chevaux-de-frise* is so called because in medieval times the people of Friesland, now the northern part of the

Netherlands, used to defend their positions with lines of sharpened wooden stakes to keep out the enemy on horseback. But our stone *chevaux-de-frise* (it occurs at three other forts in the west of Ireland) may be related to similar prehistoric ones in Spain, which suggests connections between Ireland and Spain in antiquity.

PROMONTORY FORTS

The coastline, too, was defended by the Celts. They built about 250 forts, known as promontory forts, wherever a piece of land jutted out into the sea, so that it was defended on two or three sides by the sea and by defensive ramparts on the land. The coastal promontory fort of Lough Shinny, north of Dublin city, is a good example on the east coast.

Then there are a few inland promontory forts, all of them in almost inaccessible places on the tops of remote mountains. The highest and most desolate locations for any hill-forts in the country are in County Kerry, one known as Caherconree, 615m up on Slieve Mish, and the other, called Benagh, on the summit of Mount Brandon. We can only wonder at the people who built them. Were these forts tribal gathering places where people went in times of danger? Or did they feel nearer to the gods up there in the mists and the clouds? We can never know for sure, and while such places keep their secrets we can appreciate them as part of the romance and mystery surrounding the Celts.

Also built on hilltops, but more accessible and certainly not built to resist attack, were the great royal sites of pagan Celtic tradition. They are Tara, Cruachain, Dún Ailinne, and Emain Macha. These were the legendary power-centres of the kings and heroes of our great Celtic epics and sagas. Current excavations are showing that they were also great ceremonial centres for pagan ritual in prehistoric Ireland.

Tara

Tara is probably the best known of these royal sites. It was already a sacred place by the time the Celts arrived – the Mound of the Hostages being a Stone Age burial site dating back to around 2000 BC. The Mound of the Hostages stands inside the most extensive monument on the hill of Tara – Rath na Ríogh, which means the 'Rath or Fort of the Kings'. This is a great banked enclosure which encircles the hilltop. Where this fort and the other royal sites differ from

Tara, Co. Meath, the most famous royal site in Ireland.

20

An excavation at Tara - the Mound of the Hostages.

ordinary hillforts is in having a deep ditch *inside* the bank or rampart where it would have been useless in repelling invaders. So, they cannot have been built for defensive purposes. It is possible that the internal ditch was there to keep evil spirits out of this pagan sanctuary which was the symbolic centre of Ireland in late prehistoric centuries.

Within the fort of Tara, as well as the Mound of the Hostages, there are two conjoined ringforts, one of them known as Teach Chormaic (Cormac's House). Cormac Mac Airt was one of the legendary kings of Ireland around the time of Christ. Many of the other monuments on the hill of Tara are also named after various personages from the great Irish epics, such as Rath Ghráinne (Gráinne's Fort) and Rath Meadhbha (Maeve's Fort). Gráinne was the daughter of Cormac Mac Airt, and, in the famous story 'The Pursuit of Diarmaid and Gráinne', she it was who stole away from Tara with her lover Diarmait Ó Duibhne, with Fionn Mac Cumhaill, the Celtic warrior, and the Fianna in hot pursuit.

Cruachain

Queen Meadhbh (Maeve) was, of course, Maeve of the *Táin Bó Cuailgne* (The Cattle Raid of Cooley), the best-known Irish epic of all. Queen of Connacht, Maeve was closely connected with Tara and also with another very extensive and ancient site, Cruachain in County Roscommon. This was the pagan centre of Connacht power. There are mounds and earthworks scattered over miles of countryside here, the legendary headquarters of the warrior-queen Maeve and her husband Ailill. It was from Cruachain that Maeve's great army set out for Ulster to claim the bull of Cooley, giving rise to the famous battle in which Cúchulainn defended Ulster alone against Maeve's warriors. The power-base of the Ulster kingdom was a place known as Emain Macha.

Emain Macha

Emain Macha is a huge mound on a hilltop encircled by a bank, nowadays with a nearby interpretative centre recounting the story of the hillfort in excellent detail. Like Tara, it too has an internal ditch. Here, according to legend, lived

Emain Macha, the royal fort of the kings of Ulster.

Concobhair (Conor) Mac Nessa, the jealous king of Ulster who played a major role in the tragic story of Deirdre and the Sons of Uisneach. This is the place, too, connected in people's minds with stories about Cúchulainn and with the tales of the Red Branch Knights.

Emain Macha has been brilliantly excavated and its role as a centre of pagan Celtic ritual brought to light. Emain Macha was already an ancient place of importance when the Celts of the Iron Age built a massive circular building in the huge enclosure. Inside this building they erected five circles of upright timber posts. At the centre stood one enormous timber post, which turned out to be very important to us because archaeologists have been able to date it to around the year 100 BC.

Then, very strangely, the great building was covered over with a layer of stones and a mound of earth and the outer timbers were set on fire, thus destroying most of the structure, doubtless as part of a ritual. Another aspect of this ritual was also carried out in a nearby lake, Loch na Séad (Loughnashade), into which various objects such as trumpets were thrown (Loch na Séad means 'the lake of the treasures').

Dún Ailinne

Another similar structure was built on a hilltop site known as Dún Ailinne, or Knockaulin, in County Kildare. This, too, was built within a great circular bank with a ditch on the inside, leading us to believe that here in Leinster there was another great Celtic ceremonial site built sometime close to the time of the birth of Christ.

The Celts were very preoccupied with such structures towards the end of the last millennium BC. There must have been major tribal efforts at work to build such enormous communal buildings. It was around this time too that the southern borders of Ulster were being defended with great earthworks like the ramparts of a hillfort, such as the Black Pig's Dyke on the south-western border between Ulster and Connacht, and the Dorsey on the south-eastern border between Ulster and Leinster. And in the midlands of Ireland a great roadway has been excavated dating from the same era, possibly part of a route connecting the royal site of Cruachain in Connacht with places east of the Shannon.

RINGFORTS

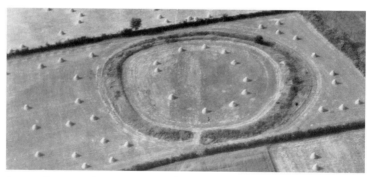

Lismore Fort, a ringfort in Co. Louth. The haystacks give an indication of the scale.

But where did the ordinary people live while all these great communal structures were in use? The answer is that we don't know, because people must have lived in flimsy structures which left no traces that can be seen today. But as time went on, farming methods changed and with the coming of Christianity, new, improved methods came to Ireland through contact with Europe. A new type of plough arrived and people tilled the ground more easily and tended to stay settled in the same place. Individual farmsteads became the norm and by the fifth century AD, many farming families were living in what are known as ringforts.

A reconstructed ringfort built at Craggaunowen, Co. Clare. The Craggaunowen project is an attempt to reconstruct dwellings similar to those of the Celtic period.

These were isolated farmsteads scattered throughout the country. Though generally called forts, they were not really designed for defence. A ringfort is a farmstead which consists of an earthen or stone circular bank sometimes with a ditch on the outside, enclosing a house and farm buildings. Different Irish terms were used for the forts; those surrounded by an earthen bank were commonly called *rath*, *dún* or *lios*, while the terms *cathair* and *caiseal* were used for those with stone walls. Townlands throughout Ireland take their names from the local prominent *dún* or *lios*, or by whatever name a particular ringfort was known. So we find placenames like Caiseal Mór (great ringfort) or Dún Beag (little ringfort) in most counties.

Ringforts varied greatly in size. They were usually forty to fifty metres in diameter, though some could be as much as a hundred metres across. The surrounding bank of earth or stone would have been quite high and possibly topped with a wooden fence. There was only one entrance to the fort and that would have been closed at night. The dwelling house and storage buildings would have been inside the fort and some of the land outside would have been cultivated. The animals would probably have been brought inside at night to keep them safe from prowling wild animals and from thieves.

The dwelling houses in the forts were usually circular. Walls were made of wood or wattle, and the roof was supported on wooden poles and probably thatched with straw, reeds or rushes. The fire was usually located in the centre, with a hole left in the roof for the smoke to escape. There were no separate rooms; bedding would simply have been spread around the walls at night, though in richer homes there may have been some partitions or screens to give privacy. People slept on piles of straw and rushes, covered with rugs and skins, the hairier skins probably being most desired to keep out cold. There would have been little furniture apart from a few wooden trestles, stools and cooking utensils.

Underground passages, or souterrains, have been found in some of the forts. Their exact purpose is uncertain but they might have been used as a hide-out in times of danger or as places for storing food.

The remains of about forty-five thousand ringforts are found throughout Ireland. Folklore says that they are the homes of the 'little people', and some people still refer to them as 'fairy forts' and regard them as magic places where humans are not really safe.

A souterrain at Craggaunowen, Co. Clare.

A Celtic nobleman or king would have had a much larger ringfort than an ordinary farmer. Not only would the house itself have been larger – the laws of hospitality demanded that all visitors be provided with accommodation and meals, and obviously a king would need to accommodate many visitors – but more land would have been enclosed to provide space for sports and training for battle, as well as for the animals. The king would have needed a strong ringfort that could be defended from his enemies. In a royal fort someone would always have been on watch to guard the entrance and keep a lookout for enemies and troublemakers.

CRANNÓGS

Ringforts were not the only type of dwelling in ancient Ireland. Some people lived on *crannógs*, which were artificial islands made in the middle of lakes or bogs. These islands were made of layers of different materials, usually

A reconstructed *crannóg* at Craggaunowen, Co. Clare.

peat and brushwood, but logs, stones, straw, rushes and animal bones were also used. The *crannógs* would then have been fenced around with timbers, with additional timbers driven into the foundations to hold the different layers together. One or two houses of daub and wattle, and pens for animals, would have been built in the *crannóg*.

The remains of over two hundred *crannógs* are still in existence throughout the country and several have been excavated, including the royal *crannóg* at Lagore in County Meath and another at Rathinaun in Lough Gara, County Roscommon.

INSIDE A CRANNÓG

Each *crannóg* seems to have been the home of one family and its dependants, rather than a group of families. The

inhabitants were probably farmers whose land lay on the surrounding shores of the lakes on which their dwellings were built. A *tóchar*, or causeway, was sometimes built from the land out to the *crannóg*, but canoes or *currachs* were the chief means of transport – canoes made from hollowed-out tree trunks have been found at some of the sites; *currachs* were made by stretching skins over a wooden frame. The *crannógs* tended to be rather damp due to their situation, consequently the moisture in the ground has preserved many objects which would have completely decayed under drier conditions. Archaeologists have discovered wood and leather

objects and even the remains of fabric. Objects such as clay crucibles and iron tongs that were used in the smelting of bronze and iron have also been discovered, evidence that the inhabitants of the *crannóg* made their own weapons and tools.

A house being built in a *crannóg*, Craggaunowen, Co. Clare.

TRAVEL

People did not usually travel very far from home in ancient times as many ordinary people did not have a horse and fewer still had any kind of cart. But paths and tracks grew along the routes people used near their homes on a regular basis. Animals made tracks and many pathways developed, for instance from driving cattle. *Bóthar,* the most common word for road in Irish today, comes from the word *bó* (a cow) and the word suggests the meaning: 'the way the cows go'.

People were expected to try and keep the roads in reasonable condition. An old Irish text stated:

> A road of whatever class must be cleared on at least three occasions, that is, the time of horse racing, winter and war.

In boggy areas, causeways made out of layers of trees, brushwood, earth and stones were sometimes built. Similarly, wooden bridges or ferryboats would have been used to cross rivers, although people usually simply waded across at shallow fords.

For at least three millennia before the arrival of the Celts, people had been making paths through the forests, bogs and marshes. The midlands of Ireland were covered by vast bogs and marshlands, and people farmed the islands of dry ground in between. But all the time the bogs were growing and it was essential for people to have a safe means of crossing them.

Archaeologists in recent years have discovered hundreds of trackways under the boglands. The preservative qualities in bogs allow for organic material like timber to survive. Some of these tracks go back to the fourth millennium BC when people started to make wooden causeways across the bogs. Simple trackways were made by throwing down layers of brushwood or hurdle tracks, similar to wattle, were made and laid down to make a safe walking surface.

Iron Age roadway at Corlea, Co. Longford.

The Celts continued this practice and made the most remarkable roads of all. Recent excavations in County Longford have uncovered the immense Corlea roadway, which ran across the bog for two kilometres. It was built of enormous oak planks laid on birch runners. The trees used in this road were felled in AD 148, which places it near enough in time to the other great construction works going on in the country, like the great temple at Emain Macha. It is the largest Iron Age roadway in Europe, big enough to take wheeled transport (and the remnants of a cart were found beneath it), but mysteriously it shows no signs of wheel ruts. So, the Corlea roadway is yet another of the unsolved enigmas of the Celtic Iron Age. It may, as suggested earlier, have been part of an ancient route between Cruachain, west of the Shannon, and Tara and Uisneach, to the east.

CHAPTER 3

POLITICAL ORGANISATION

Celtic Ireland was divided into about 150 individual king-
doms, called a *tuath*, and the people within each *tuath* were
divided into four main groups: the king, or *rí tuaithe*, and
his family, the nobles, the freemen and the unfree. Each
tuath had its own king who would lead the people into
battle and represent them in peacetime. The nobles were
land-owning families and warriors, but druids, poets and
some of the craftsmen also belonged to this group. The ordinary freemen were mainly farmers, and beneath them were
the 'unfree people' or slaves and bondsmen. A number of
tuatha, joined or allied together, made up a local province
which was ruled by a greater king. There were kings for different provinces but there was no high king, or king of all
Ireland, although some ambitious kings, around the eighth
century, tried to claim this title.

THE FAMILY GROUP

The family group was more important than any one individual in the *tuath*. In law the family group, known as the

deirbhfhine, extended to four generations and included all the descendants of a common great-grandfather. Land was owned jointly by the *deirbhfhine* and they would all have a share in any inheritance.

FOSTERAGE

Fosterage (*altramas*), a practice which seems unusual to us nowadays, was an important aspect of Celtic life. Instead of being raised at home, a child would be sent to be brought up by another family. In this way he or she would acquire a foster father and mother, and foster sisters and brothers. This led to close contacts between different family groupings, and possibly to a reduction in warfare between potentially warring families. In this sense it was a very important part of the political structure.

Children might be sent into fosterage when they were one year old and stay until they were considered old enough for marriage – seventeen for a boy, fourteen for a girl. Usually some kind of fees were paid for fostering. The fee was paid in land or most usually in cattle and varied according to rank. For the son of the lowest order of chief the fee was three cows, while for a king's son it might be as many as thirty. Higher fees were paid for the fosterage of girls as they were considered more troublesome.

A man was expected to care for his foster children as if they were his own family and to educate them for their place in life. In return, children were expected to help and support their foster parents in difficult times.

The children of noble families were carefully educated; boys were taught riding, swimming and the use of weapons, girls sewing and embroidery. Children of lesser rank were taught to work on the land and in the house – herding and farmwork for boys, using the quern and kneading for girls.

These extracts from old Irish law show some of the regulations regarding fosterage:

> How many kinds of fosterage are there? Two: fosterage for affection and fosterage for payment.

> The price of fosterage for the son of a chief is three sets; four sets is the price of fosterage of his daughter (a 'set' was half the value of a milch cow).

> There are three periods at which fosterage ends: death, crime and marriage.

The laws laid down strict regulations about the type of food that children should be given. This varied according to rank:

> Stirabout is given to them all; but the flavouring which goes into it is different. Salt butter for the sons of inferior grades, fresh butter for the sons of chieftains and honey for the sons of kings.

> Stirabout made of oatmeal or buttermilk or water is given to the sons of the *feini* grades, and a bare self sufficiency of it merely, and salt butter for flavouring. Stirabout made on new milk is given to the sons of the chieftain grades and fresh butter for flavouring, and a full sufficiency of it is

given to them and barley meal upon it. Stirabout made on new milk is given to the sons of kings, and wheaten meal upon it and honey for flavouring.

CHOOSING A KING

Although in theory any member of the royal *deirbhfhine* could be king, the *tuath*, or the whole tribe, chose the person best suited for the role, one who could lead them in battle in time of war and manage their affairs in peacetime. There were two main requirements which any would-be king had to fulfil: he was not to have any deformities or blemishes which might prevent him being a good warrior or which might make people laugh at him, and his father and grandfather must have been nobles. Though it was supposed to be a peaceful affair, rivals would often try to maim or kill each other to try and get the kingship for themselves.

THE KING

The king was a very important figure in Celtic society. He was responsible for any negotiations, either friendly or hostile, with other kings, although he did not make the laws or usually act as judge. The people believed that the rule of a good king would make the *tuath* prosperous – the crops would grow well, the seas and rivers would be full of fish, men and animals would be fertile and there would be plenty of food. If the king was unjust there would be war and famine. He had many different roles to fill within society – he was warrior, benefactor, chief justice and more, as evidenced by this extract from the laws:

The Lia Fáil, the great inauguration stone of the kings of Tara.

There are seven occupations for a king; Sunday for drinking ale, for he is not a lawful chief who does not distribute ale every Sunday; Monday for judgement, for the adjustment of the poor; Tuesday at chess; Wednesday seeing greyhounds coursing; Thursday at marriage duties; Friday at horse racing; Saturdays at giving judgements.

To challenge or disobey the decisions of the king was a dangerous undertaking, even if the decision were made on a whim with no apparent reason. The following extract from a peculiar and unusual Celtic story illustrates this.

Eating a Mouse Includes Its Tail

'Well now,' said the king, 'kill me a batch of mice.' Then he put a mouse in the food served to each man, raw and bloody, with the hair on, and this was set before them; and they were told they would be killed unless they ate the mice. They grew very pale at that. Never had a more distressing vexation been put upon them. 'How are they?' said the king. 'They are miserable, with their plates before them.' … 'Tell them they shall be killed unless they eat.' 'Bad luck to him who decreed it,' said Lughaidh, putting the mouse in his mouth while the king watched him. At that all the men put them in. There was one poor wretch of them who gagged as he put the tail of the mouse in his mouth. 'A sword across your throat,' said Lughaidh, 'eating a mouse includes its tail.'

(author unknown, ninth-tenth century)

SLAVES

Slaves were kept in some Celtic households but they were relatively few in number and certainly not to be found in every family group. They were mainly captives taken in battle and were probably kept as servants in noble households. They would have been given the heavy, difficult work to do – ploughing, sowing and harrowing for men and domestic duties for women, especially grinding corn with the quern. Slave chains have been found in excavations and there seems to have been some trade in slaves. Slave-trading

Hostage chain, beautifully made of graduated links with a decorated, hinged, iron collar. As Irish literature indicates, hostages were commonly given as a surety of good behaviour by one king or chieftain to another. This chain was found in the royal *crannóg* of Lagore near Dunshaughlin, Co. Meath, and dates to the seventh century.

went on across the Irish Sea as we know from the story of Saint Patrick, who was captured by Niall of the Nine Hostages and sold into slavery in Antrim. Brocessa, the mother of Saint Brigid, was a female slave. The Irish term for a female slave was *cumhal* and her value was regarded as being equivalent to that of three cows.

THE LAWS

The old Irish laws are called the Brehon Laws. These laws comprised the oral records of all social customs and traditions which were passed down from generation to generation by the poets and finally written down around the seventh century. We cannot know how effective these laws were in practice.

Fasting seems to have been one of the main ways of obtaining justice. A man who had a grievance against another would go and fast outside the defendant's house. If the defendant ignored him and refused to pay up, he lost his honour. Fasting could also be used to bring some evil on a person, or to succeed in a petition.

The laws stated that compensation had to be made for any injury done to another person. This compensation, related to the seriousness of the incident and also to the social rank of the person involved, was called an 'honour price'. Obviously, a chieftain had a higher honour price (*eiric*) than a slave, just as a druid would have a higher honour price than a farmer.

THE ROLE OF WOMEN

Women had a very important role in Celtic society and played an active part in everyday affairs. They had legal rights which included rights to own and inherit property. Queens and goddesses figure very heavily in Celtic stories. Queen Maeve may have originated as a fertility goddess, but became known as a warrior queen in stories such as the *Táin Bó Cuailgne*. Another war goddess was Macha; it was she who gave her name to Emain Macha and to many other places such as Ard Macha (Armagh). The reality of these powerful women is lost in the mists of time and doubtless was submerged by later notions which forced a passive role on women, but the Celtic way of life seems to have promoted such warrior women to a high status.

The Celts had liberal views about marriage. Though it was the general custom to have only one wife, there were exceptions and a man could have a chief wife and a second wife. If a couple did not suit each other, they could get a divorce without difficulty, by mutual consent, and there is some evidence that couples sometimes married just for a year.

The laws asserted that the 'marriageable age' for boys and girls was 'at the end of fourteen years for the daughter and at the end of seventeen years for the son'.

CHAPTER 4

FIGHTING

The Celts were a proud, brave people, quick to defend their honour and warlike in spirit. Cattle raids or disputes about the ownership of land or possessions often resulted in great feuds that could involve whole provinces. Kings were expected to be skilled at leading men in battle, and the Celtic heroes were always great warriors. Violence broke out easily as the young men, trained to use weapons from their boyhood, were always eager to demonstrate their courage and fearlessness in conflict. A second-century writer said of the Celts:

> The whole race is madly fond of war, high-spirited and quick to battle.

SINGLE COMBAT

The practice of fighting in single combat was quite common and disputes were often settled in this way. Each side would choose their bravest warrior and these two men would then fight each other to the death. Warriors were quick to fight if they thought that they had been insulted in any way.

> The Celts sometimes engage in single combat at dinner. Assembling in arms they engage in a mock battle-drill, and

mutual thrust and parry but sometimes wounds are inflicted and the irritation caused by this may lead even to the slaying of the opponent unless the bystanders hold them back.

Poseidonius

One Celtic custom, common to many people at this stage of historical development, was to cut the heads off enemies that they had slain in battle. To the Celts the head was especially sacred being, as they believed, the seat of the soul, so the heads of their enemies were carried home as trophies and often left as offerings to the gods.

WEAPONS

Swords and spears were the weapons most commonly used by the Celts, though slings, stones and battle axes were also available. Shields were usually used for protection and there are several references in literature to the Celtic warriors going naked into battle. This comment was made by Diodorus Siculus:

Iron spear head, ornamented on the blade with inlaid bronze rings, from Corofin, Co. Clare. It dates to the first century AD.

> Some of them so far despise health that they descend to do battle, unclothed except for a girdle.

The swords were generally iron in bronze scabbards. The spears had wooden shafts and metal heads and were widely used for hunting as well as fighting. The spear heads were normally leaf-shaped. The shields were made of alder wood and

covered in leather; they were usually rectangular and the hand grip in the centre was protected by an extra piece of wood.

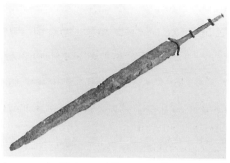

Iron sword, with bronze hilt mounts. This is a typical sword of the Celtic people who lived in Ireland. It dates to the third century AD and was found at Cashel, Co. Sligo.

On the Continent, light two-wheeled chariots were used by warriors riding into battle. There was room for two men: the warrior and the charioteer. They would drive right up to the enemy, hurling spears at them; the warrior might jump down to fight in hand-to-hand combat with his opponent, relying on his charioteer to come in and rescue him if he got into difficulties. But no remains of chariots have been found in Ireland although they do appear in epics such as the *Táin Bó Cuailgne.*

According to European sources women sometimes accompanied their husbands into battle and in some cases joined in

Sword scabbards showing typical La Tene design.

the fighting. Some women were as skilled in the handling of weapons as men, and indeed Cúchulainn was trained as a warrior by two women – Scáthach and Aoife. There are descriptions of some of these fierce women in the literature of the period. The following description was written by Ammianus Marcellinus, a Roman historian:

Almost all the Gauls are of tall stature, fair and ruddy, terrible for the fierceness of their eyes, fond of quarrelling, and of overbearing insolence. In fact a whole band of foreigners will be unable to cope with one of them in a fight, if he calls in his wife, stronger than he by far and with flashing eyes; least of all when she swells her neck and gnashes her teeth, and poising her huge white arms, begins to rain blows mingled with kicks like shots discharged by the twisted cords of a catapult.

Horse bits from the Celtic Iron Age period. These were often very highly decorated, indicating a society which placed a great value on activities associated with horses.

CHAPTER 5

WORK

Ringforts and *crannógs* were scattered widely throughout the country and as there were no towns or trading centres the people had to be largely self-sufficient. Everything that they needed - food, shelter, clothing, tools, weapons - they had to provide for themselves. Celtic society was not an equal society, and much of the heavy menial work would have been done by slaves or those of lesser rank. Nevertheless, it seems unlikely that the chiefs spent as much time fighting and feasting as the stories might suggest.

CATTLE

The Celts owned great herds of cattle and these were their most valued possession. Though the animals were kept mainly for their milk rather than their meat, they were one of the chief sources of food, and the whole Celtic way of life depended on them. Tons of cattle bones have been excavated at various sites such as the great *crannóg* at Lagore in County Meath. A person's wealth and social standing was measured by the number of cattle that he or she owned, and prices, wages and marriage portions were all estimated in terms of cattle. Cattle raiding was common and was the cause of many battles – the word *táin* means 'cattle raid'.

It seems likely that, due to the short supply of grass during the winter months, some of the animals were killed in the autumn and their meat salted and kept for later use. Still, herding the cattle and protecting them from other animals and from thieves would have been a year-round occupation. When a cow was killed it not only provided beef for the household, but a hide which could be used for everything from making footwear to covering *currachs*.

Even though haymaking went on in mainland Europe in the Iron Age, it was not practised in Ireland until the Early Christian era.

PIGS

Every farmer would have owned some pigs and large numbers of them roamed freely through the woodland, feeding on acorns and anything else that they could pick up. They were easy to manage because they could remain outdoors without shelter for most of the year. Pork seems to have been a very popular meat and it was always served at feasts.

These early pigs seem to have been a very vicious breed. The references to pigs in the stories and writings indicate that they were long-snouted, thin, muscular and active, always ready to attack and able to scour the country like hounds. As Diodorus Siculus remarked:

Their pigs are allowed to run wild and are noted for their height, and pugnacity and swiftness. It is dangerous for a stranger to approach them, and also for a wolf.

FISHING AND BOATS

Fish provided a valuable addition to the diet. Salmon and eels were often caught with a trident spear, but hooks, lines and nets were used as well. A single fishing net often served the needs of the entire *deirbhfhine*, or family group of rela-

A fishing harpoon

tions and any fish caught would be shared among the group.

As the countryside was thickly wooded and roads often little more than rough tracks, it must have been easier to travel by water than on land. The two main types of boat that were used were the *currach* and the dug-out canoe.

Wooden dug-out canoe. These vessels, used mainly on inland waters, were carved from the split trunk of an oak tree. They were propelled with broad-bladed wooden paddles by a paddler seated on the bottom of the canoe. They range in date from the Stone Age down to medieval times and were used to transport people, animals and goods. This example is about 3.65 metres long.

Currachs are still used in the west of Ireland today and have changed little in design. They were made by stretching hides over a wooden frame and stitching them together with leather thongs. Sometimes two or three layers of hide were used to make the boats stronger and safer.

Dug-out canoes were made in large numbers and seem to have been widely used on inland lakes and rivers. They would have provided the main means of communication between a *crannóg* and the shore. Archaeologists have found the remains of many of these canoes which vary in length from two to twenty metres. They were made from a single tree trunk, usually oak, and were shaped roughly at either end. The inside would either have been burnt out or chipped away with an axe. It seems that the bottom of the canoe was thicker than the sides as the extra weight made them easier to upright if they capsized.

HUNTING AND TRAPPING

Hunting was a major sport as well as being a necessity of life. Deer and wild boar were hunted when food was

Deer trap, made from wood. Drawing from the original in the National Museum of Ireland.

needed, but if the men were just out for a day's sport they would chase foxes and hares, or even wolves and badgers. Huntsmen seem to have moved on foot more often than on horseback, but they would always have been accompanied by packs of dogs, usually wolfhounds, if large, dangerous animals were being chased.

As well as being hunted down, deer were often caught in elaborate traps. One common method was to dig a deep pit, place a trap at the bottom and then cover the entrance with brambles; the deer would step on it and plunge down into the trap.

Birds were caught in a variety of ways, either stolen out of their nests or brought down in flight by a stone thrown from a sling. In coastal areas men were sometimes lowered down a cliff face in a basket tied to a rope, so that they could collect eggs and chicks from the nests.

HOUSEWORK

Much of the routine work about the house was done by the women. One of the main jobs was the preparation of food, often a slow task, especially as the corn used for bread and porridge had to be ground by hand. The small hand mills that were used for this purpose were called querns. They were quite simple in design: two stones,

Quern stone. This is the upper part of a quern used about the first century for grinding corn. Note the wooden handle (a modern reconstruction), inserted into the stone. This is an example of the 'bee-hive' type of quern.

the bottom one slightly convex in shape, the upper one concave, were fitted on top of each other, and corn was poured

in between them through a hole in the top stone; then a handle was fitted in position and pushed around so that the top stone moved over the bottom one. In this way the corn was ground into flour which fell out around the sides of the quern. This rotary quern was a Celtic invention; in the earlier type of quern, called a 'saddle quern', a round stone was merely pushed back and forth over a pile of grain placed in the bottom of a hollow stone. Though most of the grain used would have been ground by hand at home, it is probable that there were a few mills in use. The earliest type was a horizontal water mill, in which a chute of water was directed against the wheel which turned the millstones.

FOOD

Large cauldron, made of thin bronze plates riveted together. This is the sort of vessel frequently referred to in early Irish literature and it could have been used for boiling meat. From Lack East, Co. Clare, it dates to about the fifth century and is about 52 cms wide.

Milk, cheese and meat formed the main part of the Celtic diet. Bread does not seem to have been eaten in large quantities, but corn was used to make a variety of porridges. Cattle were kept for their milk rather than their meat. Beef was eaten but the animals slaughtered for this purpose would be old or maimed cows or unwanted bull calves. Pork seems to have been the main meat eaten at feasts, but mutton and venison were eaten as well.

Milk was an important foodstuff and was consumed in large quantities; it might be drunk fresh, allowed to go sour and eaten as curds, or used to make a variety of cheeses and butter. Porridge was made in many different ways, using grain from oats, barley or wheat. It was mixed with fresh or sour milk, flavoured with honey, salt or herbs, made very thick or almost liquid, and could be eaten hot or cold.

Fish were caught in the rivers and lakes and cooked over the fire. The salmon was the most prized of all fish, but trout, sea fish and shell fish were all eaten as well.

There is little evidence in the literature about the vegetables that were eaten, and people probably relied on those that they could gather in the wild rather than growing them themselves. They probably used onions, wild leeks, sorrel, nettles and watercress. A variety of fruits could have been gathered in the summer: sloe, wild cherry, raspberry, blackberry, strawberry, rowan, crabapple and elderberries, but apples seem to have been the only fruit that was cultivated in any way.

COOKING

The main way of cooking food was over an open fire; archaeologists have not found remains of ovens in the house sites. Meat was roasted on a spit over the fire, or made into a stew in a cauldron. Bread could be put to bake on a hot flagstone

Rathlogan, Co. Kilkenny. There is a *fulacht fiadha* in the raised area between the bushes. These cooking spots were usually located near flowing water.

in front of the hearth. However, the iron or bronze cooking cauldrons would have been valuable possessions, not easily available, so other methods of preparing food were devised. Remains of ancient cooking places known as *fulachta fiadha* show that hot stones were used to heat water and roast meat. A hole dug in the ground for the purpose would be filled with water which was brought to the boil by adding stones which had been heated in the fire, meat could then be put in the hole to cook.

In recent years archaeologists held an experiment at a *fulacht fiadha* at Ballyvourney in County Cork. It held 500 litres of water and the archaeologists found that this amount could be brought to the boil in thirty minutes by adding stones which had been heated in the fire. Once the water was boiling they only had to add another stone at intervals to keep up the temperature. They cooked a leg of mutton perfectly by wrapping it in straw and then boiling it for three and a half hours in this trough. Meat could be roasted by placing the joint on a hot stone and covering it with a mound of hot stones.

Once prepared, the food would have been served simply, possibly in a common bowl or dish. Drinking vessels and bowls were usually made from wood, which was easily obtainable, rather than metal. Wicker baskets could have been used to hold food as well.

WEAVING

The woollen cloth used to make cloaks and tunics would have been woven in the home. First, the wool was spun into thread, using a spindle whorl. These threads were then woven into cloth. Simple looms were made from branches and the strands of wool would have been weighted down with heavy stones. The Celts were fond of brightly coloured clothes so the fabrics would have been dyed with a variety of vegetable dyes and stains before they were made into garments. Saffron made a

A nineteenth-century reconstruction drawing of prehistoric people spinning and weaving.

yellow dye for tunics, seaweeds and lichens would produce purple and reddish colours. Some of the clothes would probably have been embroidered by the women.

CARING FOR THE SICK

It was a well established tradition among the Celts to provide special care for those who were sick. According to law a person who had wounded another had to take the victim into his own house and look after him until he was fully recovered. But certain people were not entitled to sick maintenance (*othrus*):

> There are three men in the territory who have no right to either nursing or fines: a man who refuses hospitality to every class of person, a man who is false to his honour, a man who steals everybody's property – men who do not observe their just obligations.

The laws also gave guidelines as to how the sick were to be treated and the food that they were to receive:

> Let there be proclaimed what things are forbidden in regard to him who is on his sick bed of pain. There are not admitted to him into the house fools or lunatics, or senseless people or half wits or enemies. No games are played in the house. No tidings are announced. No children are chastised. Neither women nor men exchange blows. No hides are beaten. There is no fighting. He is not suddenly awakened. No conversation is held across him or across his pillow. No dogs are set fighting in his presence or in his neighbourhood outside. No shout is raised. No pigs grunt. No brawls are made. No cry of victory is raised nor shout in playing games. No shout or scream is raised.

There are three condiments which the rule of nursing in Irish law excludes: every salt fare which is prepared with sea produce, the flesh of a whale and of a horse, and honey. For the produce of the sea impels one to drink. Does not horse flesh stir up sickness in the stomach of wounded heroes? Stomachs endure not a storm save people who can retain it. It is not right to give horse flesh to any invalid. Honey disturbs the stomach in which there is looseness of the bowels.

FEASTING

A feast was an occasion for great celebration and rejoicing, though it could often end in bloodshed as well if a warrior thought that he was not being treated with the appropriate courtesy. Men and women usually sat around in a circle at a feast, taking their places beside the chief according to rank. The champion warrior was given the best portion of meat, an honour which often resulted in fighting to decide who should receive this reward. Particular joints of meat were reserved for certain individuals at a feast, for example, a leg

A feasting cup; according to stories, this would have been passed around from person to person at the feast.

of pork for a king, a haunch for a queen, a boar's head for a charioteer.

Poseidonius, a writer who was working between 135 BC and 51 BC gave this description of Celtic feasts:

> The Celts sit on dried grass and have their meals served on wooden tables raised slightly above the earth. Their food consists of a small number of loaves of bread together with a large amount of meat, either boiled or roasted on charcoal or on spits. They partake of this in a cleanly but leonine fashion, raising up whole limbs in both hands and cutting off the meat, while any part which is hard to tear off they cut through with a small dagger which hangs attached to their sword sheath in its own scabbard ... When a large number dine together they sit around in a circle with the most influential man in the centre ... Beside him sits the host and next on either side the others in order of distinction ... The drink of the wealthy classes is wine imported from Italy or from the territory of Marseilles ... The lower classes drink wheaten beer prepared with honey, but most people drink it plain ... They use a common cup, drinking a little at a time, not more than a mouthful, but they do it rather frequently.

CHAPTER 6

A CELTIC STORY

The following story is typical of ancient Irish story-telling, and draws heavily on the Celtic way of life. It has many similarities to the *Táin Bó Cuailnge* in which Queen Maeve of Connaught fought King Conor of Ulster over possession of the bull of Cooley. In both stories the enemies are the same: Connacht and Ulster. In both the prized possession – the hound and the bull – is killed in the end and nobody actually wins despite all the killing.

MAC DATHO'S PIG

Mac Datho was a lord of Leinster and his fort was one of the five chief hostels in Ireland. The others were – the hostel of De Derga at Donnybrook, near Dublin; Forgall Monach beside Lusk; Da Res in Breffni and Da Choga in West Meath. Each hostel had seven doors; seven roads led to it; there were seven hearths and seven cauldrons on each hearth.

An ox and a salted pig went into each cauldron. The traveller who came to the hostel was told to thrust the flesh fork into the cauldron. Whatever came up at the first thrust, that was the share. If nothing came up at the first thrust the wayfarer went hungry.

Mac Datho was a very hospitable man so he was well fitted to be in charge of a hostel. He had a famous hound, called Ailbe, which could run all around Leinster in a day and a boar which was the largest in the world.

One day a messenger came from Queen Maeve of Connacht, asking Mac Datho to sell the hound. Maeve offered six hundred milch cows, a chariot with two of the best horses in Connacht and at the end of the year as much again.

'That is a good offer!' said Mac Datho politely. But he was fond of the hound and did not want to part with it. As he sat considering, another messenger arrived – this time from King Conor of Ulster. And he brought an offer for the hound.

'Conor of Ulster offers as much as Maeve of Connacht and as well, the friendship and alliance of Ulster.'

'That is also a good offer!' said Mac Datho.

But still he could not bear to part with his hound. For three days he did not eat while he thought and thought what he should do. At night he could not sleep for grieving over the loss of Ailbe and the fear that whatever he did, worse would happen. And he did not know who to ask for advice.

His wife was sorry for him.

'What ails you?' she asked. 'You won't eat the good food that's put before you and you spend the night tossing and turning instead of sleeping.'

'There's a saying,' said Mac Datho crossly, 'never trust a slave with money, nor a woman with a secret.'

'You're not getting much comfort from your wisdom!' retorted his wife. 'I might be able to settle your trouble.'

Mac Datho had never known her to give foolish counsel, so he told her the whole story.

'You see the fix I'm in? Whichever one I refuse, will take my cattle and slay my people!'

'That's not so easily settled,' agreed Mac Datho's wife. 'Whatever you do, you can't keep the hound – that's for sure! So give it to both of them and say they must come and fetch it. If there is any fighting to be done, let them fight each other. It's the best advice I can give you, and bad's the best!'

Mac Datho thought it good advice and obeyed his wife. He sent for Queen Maeve's messenger and said to him: 'It's taken me a long time to make up my mind. Now I've decided to give the hound to Connacht. But Maeve and her husband, Ailill, must come themselves with their warriors and servants to bring it away and I'll have a feast prepared worthy of them.'

The messenger rode off delighted, thinking how pleased Maeve and Ailill would be when they heard the news.

The moment he was out of the gate, Mac Datho sent for

the Ulster messenger. 'It hasn't been easy for me to agree to give up my hound,' he told him. 'But at long last I see there's nothing else for it. Tell Conor he will be welcome here to the best feast the country has known and let him bring with him his friends and fighting men.'

Away went the Ulsterman to King Conor, and Mac Datho ordered the feast.

The great boar was killed and roasted, cakes made with nuts and honey, stewed meat and soup thickened with herbs, drink of all kinds was laid upon the tables and as the boar was carried into the hall on a shield, the guests marched in.

Conor was surprised to see Maeve and Ailill; they were even more surprised to see him. The Ulstermen and the Connachtmen sat at different tables. But Conor, Maeve and Ailill sat with Mac Datho at the high table.

Before the feast could begin, the boar had to be carved.

'That is a fine boar!' agreed Ailill. 'How shall it be divided, Mac Datho?'

Before the host could answer, Briccriu, whose great pleasure was in making quarrels, leaned forward.

'Isn't it the custom that the bravest man in the company should carve the boar?' he asked. 'All the best warriors of Ireland are here. It should be easy to decide who is the finest fighter!'

'That is a sensible arrangement!' declared Ailill.

'There are many of our Ulster lads here who have fought all

through the country,' said Conor. 'It should not be hard to choose the best man.'

Along the tables the warriors shouted the brave deeds they had done. Ulstermen glared at Connachtmen. The spears and swords still leaned against the walls below the shields, but Mac Datho knew it would not be long before they were taken up and used.

At last Ket, one of the Connachtmen, leaped from his seat and, standing over the boar, knife in hand, challenged each of the Ulstermen to match his brave deeds. One after another, they told their best fights and with every one of them Ket had a braver story to tell. He looked about him triumphantly and was about to carve the boar, when a roar of welcome came from the Ulstermen seated at the end door and in walked Conall of the Victories.

He strode up to the boar, and Conor, who had been frowning, smiled again.

'I see the feast is ready,' said Conall. 'Who is carving the boar?'

'Ket,' they told him, 'for he is the bravest here!'

'Is that so?' asked Conall.

'It is!' replied Ket. 'And you are welcome to the feast, victorious Conall!'

Conall stood before him. 'And now step away from the boar that I may carve it!' he said.

'Why should I do that?' demanded Ket.

'Because since I first took weapons in my hand I have never passed one day that I did not kill a Connachtman, nor one night when I did not make a foray on them.'

Ket bent his head. 'You are then a better man than I am,' he said. 'Take my place by the boar. But if Aluain, my brother, were here, he would match every deed of you with a better, and it is a sorrow and a shame that he is not!'

'Aluain is here!' shouted Conall, and drawing from a bag the head of Aluain he flung it at Ket.

Every man in the hostel sprang to his feet, seized spear or sword and attacked the nearest man in the hostile force. Out from the hall they swept, cutting and thrusting, until King Ailill sprang into his chariot and, with Maeve beside him, shouted to the Connachtmen to stop the foolish fight and follow.

The Ulstermen pursued them. Ailbe, the hound, excited by the tumult, raced ahead and coming up with the chariot, caught the pole in its teeth. Ailill drew rein but the charioteer raised his sword and struck at the hound with a mighty blow, cutting off its head.

So neither Connacht nor Ulster won the hound and, though Mac Datho lost it, he saved his lands and his people.

(From Tales of Enchantment *by Patricia Lynch)*

A CELTIC POEM

Here is an ancient Irish poem translated by a modern poet. It gives the flavour of Celtic attachment to the land and to all things natural.

My Story

Here's my story; the stag cries,
Winter snarls as summer dies.
The wind bullies the low sun
In poor light; the seas moan.
Shapeless bracken is turning red,
The wildgoose raises its desperate head.
Birds' wings freeze where fields are hoary.
The world is ice. That's my story.

(Translated by Brendan Kennelly)

CHAPTER 7

LEISURE

Though the routine of working, hunting and possibly fighting would have occupied most of the day, there is evidence to show that the Celts liked to enjoy themselves as well. Many everyday things could give great pleasure – a good days hunting with the dogs, a house well thatched or a cloak well made, but above all the Celts seem to have loved an evening of eating and drinking, talking and singing. Feasts for special occasions – choosing a new chieftain of the tribe, celebrating marriage – could often last several days. Poetry and storytelling were an important part of Celtic life, and evenings would be spent around a fire listening to the tales of kings and warriors, battles and triumphs. There were no written documents so the only way of learning about the past was to listen to the stories and poems. Knowledge was passed on from one generation to another in this way.

POETS

A man had to study for many years to become a poet, or *file*, because he had to learn all the traditional stories and poems by heart. However, once he had done this he became a very respected man in society. The poets would travel around the country staying with different noble families, entertaining them and also bringing news of affairs in the rest of the country. They were protected by the laws and would have been welcomed by every *tuath*, although sometimes they were feared as much as respected. As well as telling the traditional stories and poems they would make up new ones and people were often rather afraid that a poem would be made about them which would make them the laughing stock of the country.

A Roman writer, Athenaeus, made this reference to a poet:

A Celtic poet, who arrived too late, met Louernius and composed a song magnifying his greatness and lamenting his own late arrival. Louernius was very pleased and asked for a bag of gold and threw it to the poet who ran beside his chariot. The poet picked it up and sang another song saying that the very tracks made by his chariot on the earth gave gold and largesse to mankind.

The Boorish Patron
I have heard that he does not give horses
for songs of praise;
he gives what is natural to him – a cow.

(author unknown, ninth century)

GAMES

The Celts seem to have practised a number of outdoor sports such as running, jumping and ball games, as well as a form of hurling. In addition, gaming pieces and dice have been found and there are references to a board game using wooden pieces that were pegged into position. Two board games called *brandubh* and *ficheall* were being played in Ireland around the seventh century and possibly much earlier. We do not really know how these games were played, but *ficheall* is often compared to chess and the word 'chess' is used to translate it.

MUSIC

The Celts loved music and no gathering or celebration would be complete without it. They realised how music can affect the feelings and emotions – the stories often refer to the way musicians calmed individuals or lulled them into sleep.

Bronze trumpet. An example of excellent craftsmanship of the Celtic metalworkers of Ireland. The two portions are each made of sheet metal folded over and secured along the edges by a strip of metal held on the inside by tiny rivets. It dates to the second century and was found in the bed of a dried-up lake called Loughnashade just outside the bank of Emain Macha (Navan Fort) near Armagh. The trumpet is about 2 metres long.

Pipes and curved bronze trumpets were common, the trumpets probably being used on ceremonial occasions, to signal men into battle or, perhaps, to mark the arrival of an important individual. The Celts were also very fond of singing and many an evening would be passed listening to musicians and singers perform.

OGHAM

The earliest writing in Ireland probably developed about AD 300. It is called *ogham*, after Ogmios, the Celtic god of writing, and was not written on paper but carved onto stone or wood. The alphabet is made up of sets of up to five strokes, diagonally across, or on either side of a central line – the central line being the edge of a stone. The inscriptions using the writing are carved on standing stones; they begin at the bottom and climb towards the top of the stone and, if necessary, continue down on the opposite side. These standing stones seem to have been used as gravestones or memorials and to mark the boundaries of land. Usually they simply record people's names.

Ogham stone at Kilmalkedar, Co. Kerry.

CELTIC BELIEFS

The Celts were a deeply spiritual people. To them, the Otherworld, the world where the gods and the spirits lived, was a part of everyday life. The gods were everywhere and ruled every aspect of life. They had to be obeyed in all things, and people made sacrifices and had special rituals in order to pacify the gods and keep them in a good mood. Among the Celtic peoples of Europe, the gods lived in rivers, in springs, in the lakes and forests, and on the mountain-tops. Making pilgrimages to high mountain-tops was a favourite way of keeping close to the gods and holy mountains like Croagh Patrick, as it came to be known, were places of pagan pilgrimage.

Each river was dedicated to a goddess in order to ensure the fertility of the land, because rivers made the land fertile. River-names like Shannon and Boyne are derived from the names of ancient fertility-goddesses and the weapons and ornaments found in them were probably deliberately cast into the water as sacrifices to the gods.

Wells and springs were places of pilgrimage too, where people came to make special offerings to the spirits of the

72

waters. These were re-dedicated to Christian saints as Ireland received the new faith.

All across Europe, weapons such as swords and scabbards, broken or bent for ritual reasons, were piled up as sacrifices to the gods and thrown into the depths of lakes and rivers. This was the case too at the great site of La Tène in Switzerland which gave its name to this era of Celtic culture.

LUGH

The Celts had many gods, and the greatest and most gifted of them all was Lugh. He was revered all over Europe, with several cities dedicated to his name, such as Lyons and Loudon. He was the god of all the arts and crafts and of every trade, and because he was also the god of the harvest, in Ireland he gave his name to Lughnasa, the month of August, the time when the crops were ripe.

DRUIDS

The druids were in charge of all religious affairs and matters of importance. They held all knowledge of the rituals which were so important in appeasing the gods. They knew the lucky and unlucky days, they read the omens and foretold the future. Their ceremonies were often carried out in secret in sacred groves and probably involved human sacrifice.

The origins of druidism were in Anglesea in Wales and druids from Ireland, Gaul and many places in Europe learned their art there. Young men spent twenty years in training and because the Celts had no writing, they learned everything by heart.

Stone head, found at Corravilla, Co. Cavan. It dates from the second or first century and was most likely the head of a pagan god.

CELTIC FESTIVALS

The Celtic year was divided into four periods corresponding to the growth cycle of the crops, with a quarterly festival at the beginning of each.

The four periods of the year were:

SAMHAIN, the winter quarter –
November, December and January

IMBOLC, the spring quarter –
February, March and April

BEALTAINE, the summer quarter –
May, June and July

LUGHNASA, the autumn quarter –
August, September and October

Because of the Celtic belief that life grows out of darkness, the Celtic year began with the festival of Samhain when the darkness of winter was approaching. Thus the new year began in winter when nature appears dead, but when, in reality, new life is germinating in the earth. Likewise, the new day began at nightfall of the day before, so Celtic festivals were marked on the eve of the actual date.

Samhain

On the festival of Samhain, or Oíche Shamhna as it is called in Irish today, the gates of the Otherworld were open and people communicated with their ancestors. This was the night when ghosts and fairies were abroad, and when the *púca*, or færy horseman, rode out. The last of the blackberries and haws withered under his breath as a reminder that the harvest was now truly over.

According to a lovely Irish tradition, people sweep the floor and leave the fire kindled for any fairies who might be passing. In Christian times this festival came to be known as Hallowe'en (the eve of All Hallows or All Saints). It was a time that was especially dedicated to the memory of the dead and ushered in the month when people prayed for their dead and visited their graves.

Imbolc

This is a very ancient word and was probably originally *óimolg*, meaning 'ewe-milk', and is perhaps connected with the birth of the lambs. It marks the beginning of the growth cycle of the year when animals are being born and when the goddess of fertility was invoked to oversee the birth of lambs and calves to ensure a steady supply of milk for their survival.

St Brighid (Brigid) of Kildare became part of this fertility cult and is still honoured as the patroness of spring. Many traditional spring customs are still practised in Ireland today, such as the weaving of St Brighid's crosses to hang in kitchens and dairies.

Bealtaine

This festival marks the beginning of the summer season when the crops flourish in the heat of the sun. The coming of summer, marking the bright half of the year, was celebrated enthusiastically by the Celts with fires especially kindled. This was a task for the druids in ancient times. May-day customs are still observed widely in Britain and Ireland.

Lughnasa

The festival of Lughnasa, celebrating autumn, marks the fruitfulness of the field crops and ushers in the all-important season of autumn when the crops and fruits are ready for harvest and when fields and orchards are full.

Lughnasa means 'Lugh-assembly' and is named for Lugh, who was the greatest of the gods (he is often called An tIoldánach, 'The multi-skilled'). He was the patron of the harvest time when the crops are ripe in the fields.

The festival of Lughnasa was celebrated with gatherings and fairs. This was the day when people made the long climb to the highest mountain-tops to honour the harvest god. High mountains like Croagh Patrick, as it came to be known in Christian times, and Mount Brandon in Kerry were special places and became the focus of great pilgrimages when the Celts were Christianised.

The name of Lugh, and the word Lughnasa meaning 'August', still live on today and are the inspiration of Brian Friel's modern masterpiece of drama *Dancing at Lughnasa*.

This festival, now celebrated on the last Sunday in July, is known by various names in Ireland – Garland Sunday, Reek Sunday at Croagh Patrick, Frochan Sunday (in the Wicklow area blueberries are known as *frochans* and are collected at this time).

DEATH AND BURIAL

In the Celtic tradition there was a strong belief in the after-life. People felt that the dead were never far away. Cremation was widely practised, probably in the belief that the purifying properties of fire released the spirit into the after-life. This may

Bronze objects. Sometimes known as 'spoons' or 'castanets'. Their exact function is unknown. They are usually found in pairs in the graves of Celtic women. These examples date to the first century.

explain why we have very little evidence for early Celtic burial customs. Before or around the time of Christ burials did take place in 'ring barrows', small mounds enclosed by a ring of earth, which are found in various places around the country. With the coming of Christianity, burial practices became more like what we know today.

Some of the most enduring Celtic traditions are related to death. In Ireland today the beautiful old custom of waking the dead is still with us. Friends and neighbours visit and pray beside the dead person, and while away the long hours of the night keeping the dead person company on his or her long journey to the after-life.

The lonely cry of the banshee (*bean-sí,* 'færy woman') was frequently heard. She was the death messenger and her high-pitched cry announced a forthcoming death.

Celtic people honoured their dead by expressing their grief openly. The *caoineadh,* for example, was a special lament carried out by the keeners, or keening women (*mná caointe),* who grieved aloud with the mourners and recited the dead person's life story and all the good things that the person had achieved.

CHAPTER 9

THE ART OF THE CELTS

The Celts of the La Tène period were wonderful artists. In Europe, they left behind a legacy of wealth and beauty. Warriors and chieftains wore lavishly-decorated sword-scabbards and shields. Their horses wore beautiful bridle-bits and other trappings. Men and women alike wore personal ornaments such as bracelets, finger-rings and highly decorated neck ornaments known as torcs.

The art of La Tène is an art of flowing curvilinear abstract design. It has its origins in the oak forests of Europe.

Bronze trumpet-face from Loughnashade, Emain Macha.

The Celtic people who lived in the deep shade of the vast forests were influenced by the interplay between light and shade in their everyday lives. They were so used to living with ever-changing shapes and mysterious

Bronze object, possibly a box lid, from Somerset, Co. Galway.

shadows that it was natural for them to express these shapes in their art. So the art of the La Tène Celts is playful and elusive. What appears to be a bunch of leaves or a wavy vine tendril might seem to have a human face lurking in the shadows, but when we look again, it has vanished! It reminds us of what the Greek writer Poseidonius wrote about the Celts about one hundred years before Christ:

> They speak in riddles, hinting at things, leaving much to be understood.

The Irish Celtic craftsmen of the La Tène period worked in the European tradition but they developed their own Irish style. They worked mainly in bronze and gold. (Iron was used extensively too, usually for making more everyday objects like knives, but as it corrodes over time much of it has disappeared.)

There are six beautifully engraved sword-scabbards from the Celtic Iron Age which would have been proudly worn by Irish chieftains two centuries before the birth of Christ. They were found buried in a bog in County Antrim. There are several bronze horse-bits from various parts of Ireland, some beautifully ornamented like that from Attymon in County Galway. Many of these high-status objects, like swords and scabbards, have been recovered from watery places like rivers, lakes and bogs, suggesting that they were thrown in as offerings to the gods.

A beautifully-ornamented bronze trumpet-face came from the lake known as Loch na Séad (the Lake of the Treasures) beside the great fort of Emain Macha. Some of the great carved stones from the Celtic Iron Age, such as the Turoe Stone in County Galway

Ornamental disc, about 25cm in width, with raised patterns beaten from the bronze base.

(illustrated on the cover of this book), are lavishly decorated in the La Tène style. Such stones must have been the focus of mysterious rituals in the out-of-doors. Indeed, the curving designs of the La Tène art style probably had a symbolic or religious meaning, now lost to us.

In gold, the most spectacular find is the Broighter hoard. It consists of several pieces of personal ornament, among them a truly splendid torc, lavishly ornamented, and a tiny boat with a mast and oars.

The art of the Celts grew and changed over the centuries. Christianity, when it arrived in the fifth century AD, brought new momentum and new skills which became grafted onto the old Celtic style. In metalwork, in stone and in manuscripts, the Christian Celtic artistic tradition flourished, producing, by the eighth century, such masterpieces as the Ardagh chalice, the Book of Kells and the magnificent high crosses.

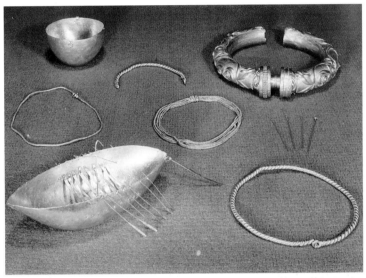

Hoard of gold objects found together by two ploughmen at Broighter, near Limavaddy, Co. Derry. Included are a beaten sheet gold bowl; three fine necklaces and a portion of a fourth; and a superb example of early Irish craftsmanship in the form of a hollow gold collar, the whole surface of which is decorated with raised designs. There is also a small boat complete with steering oar, fourteen rowing oars, seats for oarsmen and mast. The hoard dates to the first century and can be seen in the National Museum.

CHAPTER 10

THE BEST-LOVED CELTIC STORY OF ALL - THE CHILDREN OF LIR

One of the best-loved and most famous stories from Ireland is 'The Children of Lir'. It has many of the elements that the Celts loved in their stories: loneliness, exile, shape-changing. It shows the special relationship the Celtic people had with the animal world and the consolation they got from music. It spans that period which has always fascinated people of later times – when the pagan world met with Christian beliefs for the first time.

In the days when Ireland was inhabited by two races of people, the People of Dana or the De Danaan, and the Milesians, these two races agreed to divide the country between them so that they would no longer fight about territory.

They agreed that the Milesians would take the upper half of the country which lay above ground, and that the De Danaan would take the territory below the ground.

The De Danaans chose as their king Bov the Red who was a very wise and noble man. All his subjects were loyal to him except Lir, the father of Manannan Mac Lir, the sea-god. Lir was offended because he had not been chosen as king himself and from the day that Bov the Red became king, Lir avoided going to court and ignored him.

Some years later, Bov the Red sent for Lir and asked him if he would like to marry one of his three foster daughters. Bov hoped that this would give Lir a chance to forget his disappointment and become friendly once again. And indeed it did. Lir was so pleased to hear from Bov that he decided to set out immediately for the palace on the shores of Lough Derg.

Lir and his followers were given a great welcome when they arrived and a feast was prepared for them. The three foster daughters were present during the meal and when everybody had eaten the king invited Lir to take his choice of the three girls. As all three were very beautiful it was not an easy decision, but eventually he decided to choose the eldest one, Eve.

Lir and Eve were married that same day and two weeks later Lir brought his bride home to Shee Finnehy.

After some time Eve gave birth to twins, a boy and a girl whom they called Aed and Finola. Lir loved his wife and children dearly and was very happy. Two years later, Eve gave birth to another pair of twins, two sons whom they named Fiacra and Conn. But sadly, Eve died soon after their birth. Lir was heartbroken at losing her and he worried too about his children who were left without a mother.

Not long afterwards King Bov, who was sad to hear of Eve's death, sent a message to Lir asking him if he would like to marry Aoife, the second foster daughter. Lir agreed, hoping that Aoife would fill the empty place in their lives.

So Lir went again to Bov's palace, married Aoife and brought her back home with him. She looked after the children well and they loved her dearly in return. These children gave Lir great happiness, indeed he loved them so much that he liked them to sleep in a room near his own. Every morning when they awoke he played with them and told them stories. King Bov, their grandfather, was very fond of them too and they visited him frequently. They were beautiful and affectionate children, and everyone who knew them loved them.

Unfortunately, as time went on, Aoife began to resent the care that was lavished on the children. She was jealous because Lir loved them so much and felt that even her father paid more attention to his grandchildren than to her, his own daughter. Slowly her hatred for the children grew until finally she could not bear to look at them and began to plan how she could be rid of them altogether.

One day she asked for her chariot to be made ready and she called the children and told them that she was taking them to see their grandfather. So Aed, Finola, Fiacra and Conn got into the chariot with their stepmother and set out on the long journey to the palace of their grandfather.

When they reached Lake Derravaragh in the middle of Ireland, Aoife ordered everyone to get out of the chariot to allow the horses to rest and be watered whilst she brought the four children down to the lakeside to bathe. They raced down to the lake, laughing and shouting excitedly to each other, but as soon as Aoife saw that they were in the water she chanted a spell over them and touched their heads with a druid's wand. Immediately Aed and Finola, Fiacra and Conn were changed into four beautiful white swans.

When they realised what had happened these four swans looked sadly at their stepmother, and then Finola said, 'Why have you done this to us Aoife? We loved you, and we thought that you loved us. What did we do to deserve such a dreadful punishment?'

Aoife forgot her jealousy as she suddenly realised what a terrible thing she had done, but it was too late to undo the spell. The children had been condemned to a long exile, they had to spend three hundred years on Lake Derravaragh, three hundred years on the Sea of Moyle and three hundred years on Inish Glora on the Western Sea. They would remain as swans until Christianity came to Ireland. Aoife tried to lessen the suffering she had caused them by promising that, though outwardly they would have a swan's shape, their personalities would remain unchanged. They would still be able to talk and to make music. Then Aoife got back into her chariot and continued her journey to her father's house. The four swans were left behind on the lake.

King Bov was surprised to see her arrive alone, especially when she said that Lir had not allowed the children to come with her, but he soon heard the true story. When he realised what had happened to his grandchildren he was heartbroken, and as a punishment for her wicked deed he turned Aoife into a demon spirit that would find no rest on the earth.

Afterwards Bov the Red, Lir and some of the nobles went to the shores of Lake Derravaragh. They made camp there so that they could be near the swans and keep them company. In this way the next three hundred years on Lake Derravaragh passed pleasantly – the swans had friends around them and were able to spend the days talking and making music – music so beautiful that it charmed everyone who heard it.

Finally, however, the time came for them to move on to the Sea of Moyle. Aed and Finola, Fiacra and Conn were sad to leave because they had been almost as happy on Lake Derravaragh as they had been as children at home, but they could not avoid the spell that had been placed on them.

Early one morning, having spoken to their father and friends for the last time, the swans sang a beautiful song in farewell and then flew away from the lake, north towards the Sea of Moyle.

However, their spirits sank into despair when they arrived on the Sea of Moyle – it was cold and stormy and the only company they had there were the shrieking sea-gulls and the seals. They missed their friends and they seldom talked or sang. They spent many lonely days and nights in this uninhabited place but, at last, the three hundred years passed and it was time to move to Inish Glora.

They arrived at Inish Glora and landed on a small lake there. It was much more pleasant than the Sea of Moyle. The climate was quite gentle and there were thousands of birds in the area, birds that gathered to listen to the swans when they were singing their sad laments for their lost childhood, and for their father long dead, and for the home they once knew that now lay in ruins.

By this time St Patrick was travelling throughout the country preaching to the people and building churches and monasteries to spread the Christian faith across the land. One of his followers, a man called Kemoc, built a church on Inish Glora. One morning, soon after he arrived, the four children of Lir were woken up by the sound of the church bell. They were terrified because they had never heard such a sound before. Finola finally realised what it was and she was happy because she knew that this could break the spell that Aoife had put on them centuries ago. When she told the others this they began to sing with joy and the sweet sound of their music reached Kemoc who was praying in his church on the far side of the lake. He went down to the shore and spoke to the swans, asking them if they really were the children of Lir, famous throughout the country for their singing. They told him that they were indeed these children and he was able to say that the spell would soon be broken. He would look after them until it was removed.

So the swans came ashore and went to Kemoc's house and lived with him there. He told them about the teachings of Christ, and they would join him in his prayers. The days passed happily, until finally, one day, as the swans sang a sweet hymn for Kemoc, their feathers dropped off and they became human again. Finola was a frail, white-faced old woman, and her three brothers were feeble old men, grey-haired, bony and wrinkled.

The children of Lir asked Kemoc to baptise them because they felt they would die soon, and indeed they died peacefully a short time later. Kemoc buried them side by side in one grave and he wrote their names on a tombstone over the grave:

'Aed, Finola, Fiacra and Conn – the Children of Lir'

ACKNOWLEDGEMENTS

The Curriculum Development Unit thanks Áine Hyland, Anne Gill and Brian Kavanagh for work in the development of materials; Tim O'Neill for reading and commenting on the manuscript; the Editor of the Proceedings of the Royal Irish Academy for permission to quote from J.J.Tierney, 'The Celtic Ethnology of Poseidonius' (PRIA, 1960); Dr Brendan Kennelly for kind permission to include 'My Story'. We acknowledge the assistance of the late Dr Joseph Raftery, Director of the National Museum of Ireland, in the preparation of this book.

ILLUSTRATIONS

The publisher thanks the following for photographs and illustrations: National Library of Ireland, p.7; National Museum of Ireland, back cover, pp. 8, 10, 11, 12 (top), 12 (bottom), 40, 46 (top), 47, 50, 52, 54, 59, 70, 74, 78, 80, 81, 82, 83, (bottom); Department of Arts, Heritage, Gaeltacht and the Islands, front cover (bottom), back cover (background), pp. 16, 18, 20, 21, 38, 56, 71; Shannon Heritage and Banquets, pp. 2, 25, 27, 28, 30; Northern Ireland Tourist Board, front cover (top), p.22; Cambridge University Collection, p.24; Prof. Barry Raftery, p.32; Josip Lizatovic, p.46 (bottom); Jeannette Dunne, pp. 50, 51.

Other Books in the *Exploring Series*
from THE O'BRIEN PRESS

EXPLORING THE BOOK OF KELLS

George Otto Simms

Reconstruction drawings: David Rooney
Full colour reproductions from the Book of Kells

A beautiful and simple introduction to the Book of Kells. Here George Otto Simms, a world-renowned authority on the Book of Kells, reveals the mysteries hidden in this magnificent manuscript. He introduces the monks who made the book and guides the reader through the intricate detail of this ancient and exotic book. With beautiful drawings and colour photographs.

Joint winner, with *Brendan the Navigator,* of the
Irish Children's Book Trust
BOOK OF THE DECADE AWARD

Hardback £7.99/$11.95

BRENDAN THE NAVIGATOR

George Otto Simms

Reconstruction drawings: David Rooney

The story goes that fifth-century St Brendan may in fact have travelled across the Atlantic in his little skin boat all the way from Ireland to America. Volcanoes, icebergs, sea-monsters, strange beings – all these play a part in this ancient adventure story. Simms unravels the mysteries and wonders of Brendan's travels and explains why and how the voyage was undertaken.

> 'A perfect book … As with his previous bestseller (*Exploring the Book of Kells*) Simms has shone his craftsman's light of love on the world of Brendan and made it live.
> RTE GUIDE

Paperback £4.99/$7.95

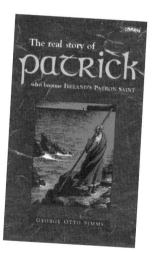

THE REAL STORY OF ST PATRICK

George Otto Simms

Reconstruction drawings: David Rooney

The real story of St Patrick, Ireland's patron saint.

Many legends, stories and traditions have grown up over the centuries about Ireland's most famous saint. George Otto Simms goes back to Patrick's own *Confession* and his other writings to separate the man from the myth. What emerges is a fascinating, true story of a man of great strength and of his adventures and trials, told in a way that will appeal to both young and old.

David Rooney's charming illustrations show St Patrick's arrival in Ireland, his powerful visions and his battles with the Druids. Early Celtic artefacts and details from the ninth-century *Book of Armagh* also illustrate the text.

'a new interpretation and explanation by a leading scholar'
LEINSTER LEADER
'charming and elegant account'
IRELAND OF THE WELCOMES

Paperback £5.99/$8.95

THE WORLD OF COLMCILLE
also known as Columba
Mairéad Ashe FitzGerald
Illustrated by Stephen Hall

Celt and Christian, prince and saint, this remarkable man from the sixth century was known as Colmcille in his native Ireland and as Columba of Iona in Scotland and to the wider world.

This book explores the life and times of this complex and powerful man who was involved in the politics, religion and art of his day. A towering figure in Early Christian times, Colmcille/Columba played a central role in the political events of sixth-century Ireland and Scotland as an advisor to kings and chieftains. He also furthered the influence of Gaelic culture in Scotland, and founded the famous monastery of Iona. As a scholar and scribe, he played an important part in the development of Early Christian art, which was to reach its greatest expression in the Book of Kells.

Hardback £8.99/$12.95 Paperback £5.99/$8.95

THE VIKINGS IN IRELAND
Morgan Llywelyn

Illustrated by David Rooney

For the first time a blend of fact and fiction by a master writer of historical fiction, telling the story of the Vikings in Ireland. Here are the details of the Viking invasions, of their eventual settlement and integration with the native Irish, their contribution to Irish life, the differences between their way of life and that of the Irish of the period. Occasional fictional inserts add spice to the story, thus giving the feelings and excitement as well as the facts of the period.

Hardback £7.99/$12.95

Send for our full-colour catalogue
These books are available from your bookseller and from our website. In case of difficulty you may order direct, using this form.

ORDER FORM

Please send me the books as marked

I enclose cheque/postal order for £ . . . . (+£1.00 P&P per title)

OR please charge my credit card ☐ Access/Mastercard ☐ Visa

Card Number __ __ __ __   __ __ __ __   __ __ __ __   __ __ __ __

Expiry Date __ __ / __ __

Name. . . . . Tel . . . .

Address . . . .

. . . .

Please send orders to : THE O'BRIEN PRESS, 20 Victoria Road, Dublin 6.
Tel: +353 1 4923333 Fax: + 353 1 4922777 e-mail: books@obrien.ie
www.obrien.ie